MW00903294

Thomas, Matt

Singapore

DUE DATE

OVERSIZE
J 915.957
T

pt. 2-5
8/09
8/08
6/06
5/05
2/03

MAR 1 1 2002

A Statue Of A Singapore Woman

FACES AND PLACES

SINGAPORE

BY MATT THOMAS

THE CHILD'S WORLD®, INC.

COVER PHOTO

A uniformed boy in Singapore.
©The Purcell Team/CORBIS

Published in the United States of America by The Child's World®, Inc.
PO Box 326
Chanhassen, MN 55317-0326
800-599-READ
www.childsworld.com

Project Manager James R. Rothaus/James R. Rothaus & Associates
Designer Robert E. Bonaker/R. E. Bonaker & Associates
Contributors Mary Berendes, Dawn M. Dionne, Katherine Stevenson, Ph.D., Red Line Editorial

Library of Congress Cataloging-in-Publication Data
Thomas, Matt.
Singapore / by Matt Thomas.
p. cm.
Includes index.
ISBN 1-56766-910-7 (lib. bdg : alk. paper)
1. Singapore—Juvenile Literature.
[1. Singapore]
I. Title.
DS609 .T47 2000
959.57—dc21

Table of Contents

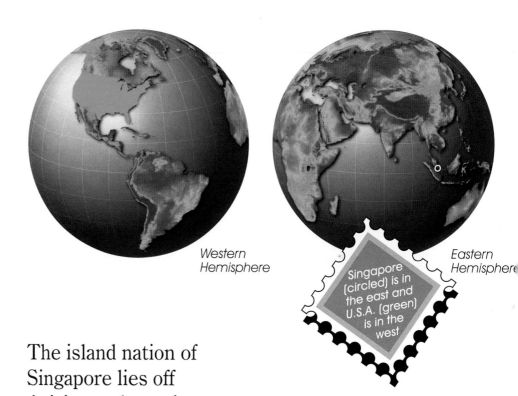

Where Is Singapore?

When most people look out a window, they can see one thing—land. But did you know that Earth has more water than land? Earth is covered with huge oceans. Within these oceans are large land areas called **continents**. The largest of Earth's continents is Asia.

Western Hemisphere

Eastern Hemisphere

Singapore (circled) is in the east and U.S.A. (green) is in the west

The island nation of Singapore lies off Asia's southern tip.

Only a narrow strip of water separates Singapore from neighboring Malaysia. A wider strip of water separates it from Indonesia.

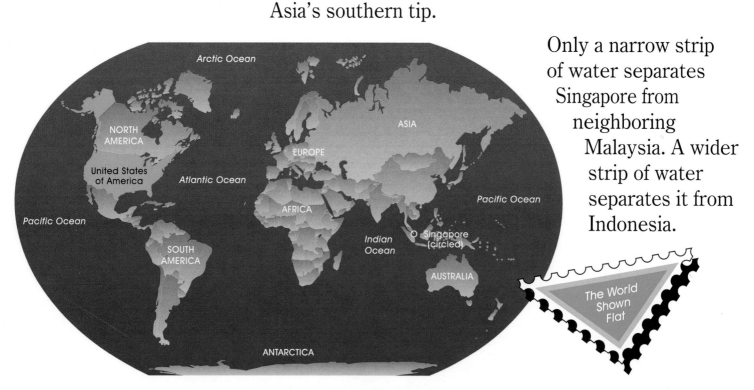

Arctic Ocean

NORTH AMERICA

United States of America

Atlantic Ocean

Pacific Ocean

AFRICA

SOUTH AMERICA

EUROPE

ASIA

Indian Ocean

Pacific Ocean

Singapore (circled)

AUSTRALIA

ANTARCTICA

The World Shown Flat

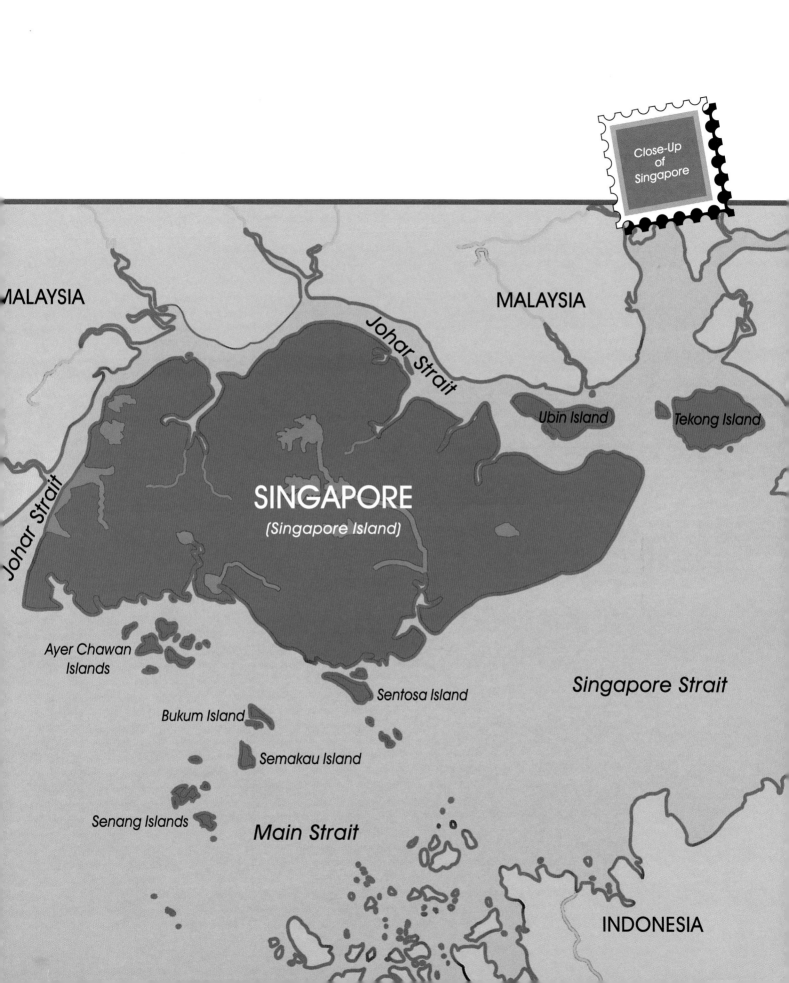

Close-Up
of
Singapore

MALAYSIA

MALAYSIA

Johar Strait

Johar Strait

Ubin Island

Tekong Island

SINGAPORE
(Singapore Island)

Ayer Chawan
Islands

Singapore Strait

Sentosa Island

Bukum Island

Semakau Island

Senang Islands

Main Strait

INDONESIA

Bukit Timah
Nature
Reserve

Bukit Timah
Nature
Reserve

Downtown
Singapore

Sentosa

©Robert Holmes/CORBIS

The Land

A View Of Downtown Singapore

©Larry Lee Photography/CORBIS

Singapore is a very small country. In fact, the whole nation could fit within the city limits of a major U. S. city! Singapore is made up of one main island and about 60 smaller islands. The middle of Singapore's main island is higher than its coasts. The entire island, however, is fairly flat.

Asian Village On Sentosa Island

©Robert Holmes/CORBIS

Singapore lies on the **equator,** an imaginary east-west line that divides the world in half. Countries near the equator have warm weather all year long. Singapore's weather is hot and sticky. **Monsoons** are the only weather change. These are times when a constant wind brings a lot of rain to the island.

At one time, the island of Singapore was covered with thick rain forests. Trees and plants grew easily in the warm, **tropical** weather. Today, most of the nation is made up of the city of Singapore, and little of the natural forest remains. Most of Singapore's remaining rain forest is in **reserves**.

When the rain forest was cut down, many of the large animals such as deer, wild boar, and tigers died out. However, smaller animals such as snakes, birds, and monkeys can still be seen in many of Singapore's nature parks. Ocean creatures such as fish and crabs still live in the islands' beautiful coral reefs.

©Bob Krist/CORBIS

A Scarlet Macaw Parrot

©Wayne Lawler; Ecoscene/CORBIS

Tropical Rain Forest In Buckit Timah National Park

Bukit Timah Nature Reserve

Blooming Mokara Plants At A Botanical Garden

©Kevin R. Morris/CORBIS

Sailing Ships
In A
Singapore
Harbor In
1880

Downtown
Singapore
and Harbor

Bust Of Sir Thomas Stamford Raffles

©Adam Woolfitt/CORBIS

Singapore got its name hundreds of years ago when a prince saw a strange-looking animal on the island. He thought the animal was a lion and named the place Singa-Pura, or "lion city."

Because of its location, Singapore has always been an important island for shipping. In the 1800s, the British sent Sir Thomas Stamford Raffles to the island to build a trading post for shipping. Within a few years, the British took control of the entire island and began to build a shipping city.

Downtown Singapore In 1941

©Bettmann/CORBIS

The British controlled Singapore until World War II, when the island was invaded by Japan. After the war, the British again took over the island, but Singapore's people were tired of being ruled by other countries. Finally, in 1965, Singapore became its own country.

Singapore Today

The Singapore Supreme Court Building

©Kevin R. Morris/CORBIS

The city of Singapore continued to grow as a trading city. Today the city takes up most of the nation's land. Most of the original forest was leveled to make room for buildings, shops, roads, and houses. Even so, Singapore's builders tried to include nature within the city. Beautiful public parks and gardens are the result.

One of the major reasons for Singapore's growth is its government. The government's actions affect every part of the lives of Singapore's people. Singapore's leaders, like those of the United States, are elected by the people.

Singapore Skyline And Harbor

©Dennis Degnan/CORBIS

Singapore's government has a president. It also has a **parliament**, a group of people who make the nation's laws. The parliament's leader is the prime minister. It is the prime minister's job to make sure everything runs smoothly.

Downtown
Singapore
and Harbor

©Michael S. Yamashita/CORBIS

A Bridge
Across A
Pond In
A Singapore
Park

Singapore Island

Chinese Opera
Singers

The People

A Young Woman In Traditional Clothes

When the British first arrived on Singapore, few people were living there. As the trading city grew, however, people from many different countries came to live there.

Today, people from three major **ethnic groups** live in Singapore. They are Chinese from China, Indians from India, and Malays from the neighboring Malay **peninsula** and its nearby islands.

A Construction Worker With Plans For An Oil Rig

Each ethnic group brought its own culture, values, and beliefs to the small island. Singapore's culture is now an interesting mixture of traditions. Singapore's people believe in working hard. They also believe in the importance of family and community.

**City Life
And
Country
Life**

Apartment Buildings In Singapore

©Dean Conger/CORBIS

Since Singapore's city occupies most of the main island, almost all of the country's people live there. As in many big cities, most Singaporeans live in **flats**, or apartments. In fact, almost nine-tenths of Singapore's people live in government-run apartment buildings.

The city of Singapore is divided into small areas with names such as Chinatown, Little India, and the Arab district. Each part of town has a special look and feel.

A Hindu Temple In Little India

©The Purcell Team/CORBIS

Singapore's people are still trying to balance nature and the city. They are also trying to balance traditional ways of life with modern city life. Ancient temples still stand, surrounded by towering new buildings.

Singapore Island

Shops In Chinatown

©Kevin R. Morris/CORBIS

Singapore Island

Schoolchildren At A Bus Stop

Offerings At A Chinese Street Altar

Education is very important to Singaporeans. No one is forced to go to school, but almost every child goes to elementary school. Most also attend secondary school. Singapore's schoolchildren learn to read, write, and do math just as you do.

People speak several different languages in Singapore's schools. In fact, Singapore has four official languages: Mandarin, Malay, Tamil, and English. All schoolchildren learn English. They also learn their parents' languages to help them remember the old traditions.

A Billboard Advertising Tiger Balm

Camera Assembly Workers

Singaporeans are a hard-working people. They work at jobs like those in any big city. Most of Singapore's people work in business or manufacturing. Because the city is so big, few people make their living by farming or fishing.

©Dean Conger/CORBIS

Net Fishing In Singapore

Singapore's factory workers make everything from pipes to clothes. Many factories make electronic equipment. Oil refineries are important as well. In fact, Singapore has one of the world's largest oil refineries.

©Michael S. Yamashita/CORBIS

Singapore Island

©Michael S. Yamashita/CORBIS

Singapore's Largest Oil Refinery

Singapore Island

A Cook
Prepares
Dim Sum
And Other
Appetizers

Food

A Woman Cooking Outdoors

Singapore's foods reflect the many different types of people who live there. *Hawker centers,* or outdoor food stands, feature almost every type of food from all around the world!

As in many Southeast Asian countries, rice is an important part of Singaporean meals. Besides rice, typical meals include a fish or meat dish, soup, and a vegetable dish. One popular dish is chilli crab, made from pieces of crab meat fried in a special sauce.

©Dean Conger/CORBIS

Fruit For Sale In Singapore's Holland Village

©Michael S. Yamashita/CORBIS

Another popular dish is *dim sum.* To make this tasty meal, bite-sized rolls are filled with different meats and vegetables.

Pastimes and Holidays

ADMIT ONE · ADMIT ONE

Many Singaporeans like to spend time picnicking or snorkeling at the beach. Others like to visit family or go shopping in Singapore's many stores.

Games and sports are also popular. One of Singapore's most popular games is **mahjong**, a card-like game played with colorful tiles. People also enjoy playing golf, cricket, and soccer, and flying beautiful kites.

Holidays and festivals are wonderful occasions in Singapore. Most of the holidays are religious. Many also celebrate important times in the Singaporean calendar, such as the Mooncake Festival or the New Year. These holidays are times for singing, dancing, food, and fireworks.

Whether you like shopping and parties, beautiful beaches, or quiet temples, a visit to Singapore is a visit you will never forget!

Ferry Passengers Pass Time Playing Mahjong

©Kelly-Mooney Photography/CORBIS

Singapore Island

©Ted Streshinsky/CORBIS

New Year Parade

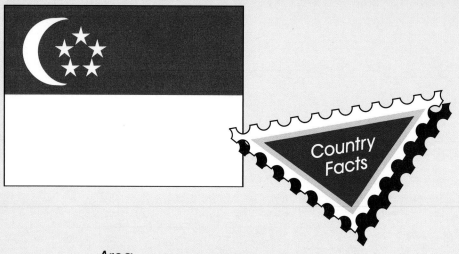

Area
About 250 square miles
(647.5 square kilometers)—about 3.5 times as big as Washington, D.C.

Population
About 3 million people.

Capital City
Singapore.

Money
The Singaporean dollar.

National Language
The official languages are Malay, English, Mandarin, and Tamil.

National Song
"Majulah Singapura," or "Let Singapore Flourish."

National Holiday
National Day on August 9th.

National Flag
Singapore's flag is half red and half white. The red part has a crescent moon and five small stars. The red stands for the equality of all people, and the white stands for goodness. The moon symbolizes the growing land, and the stars stand for democracy, peace, progress, justice, and equality.

Head of State
The president of Singapore.

Head of Government
The prime minister of Singapore.

Chinese
New Year
Decorations

Did You Know?

Singapore gets thunderstorms on more than 140 days a year. That's about three stormy days a week!

More than twice as many people visit Singapore each year than actually live there. That makes Singapore's airport and seaport two of the busiest ports on Earth.

Singapore's main island doesn't have enough fresh drinking water for everyone who lives there. It must buy water from neighboring Malaysia and ship it over by boat.

To keep its armed forces strong, Singapore requires all men over 18 years of age to spend two years in the military.

Singapore's large population needs lots of roads and subway tracks for getting from place to place. If they could be stretched out end to end, the main island's roads and subway tracks would be over 1,900 miles long. That's over 80 times the length of the entire island!

How Do You Say?

	MALAY	HOW TO SAY IT
Hello	halo	hah–LOH
Goodbye	selamat tinggal	seh–LAH–maht ting–GAHL
Please	sila	see–LEH
Thank You	terima kasih	teh–REE–meh KAH–see
One	satu	saah–TOO
Two	dua	DOO–eh
Three	tiga	TEE–geh
Singapore	Singapore	SING-ah-poor

continents (KON-tin-nents)
Earth's land areas are divided into huge sections called continents. Singapore is part of the continent of Asia.

equator (ee-KWAY-ter)
The equator is an imaginary line around the middle of Earth, halfway between the North and South Poles. Singapore and other countries near the equator have warm weather all year.

ethnic groups (ETH-nik GROOPS)
An ethnic group is a group of people who have the same customs, language, ideas, and ways of life. Three major ethnic groups live in Singapore.

flats (FLATS)
A flat is another name for an apartment. Most of Singapore's city dwellers live in flats.

mahjong (mah-ZHONG)
Mahjong is a tile game that's a little like cards. Players draw from 144 tiles until they get a winning hand.

monsoons (mon-SOONZ)
Monsoons are winds that bring heavy rains to countries in southern Asia and the Indian Ocean. Monsoons provide the only real weather change in Singapore.

parliament (PAR-luh-ment)
In some countries, laws are created by a group of elected people called a parliament. Singapore has a parliament.

peninsula (peh-NIN-soo-luh)
A peninsula is an area of land that is almost entirely surrounded by water. Singapore's neighbor, Malaysia, lies on the Malay Peninsula.

reserves (ree-ZERVZ)
Reserves are areas of land set aside to protect animals and nature. Most of the rain forest still left in Singapore lies within reserves.

tropical (TROP-ih-kull)
A tropical area has warm weather all year long. Plants grow well in Singapore's tropical weather.

Index

Web Sites

Learn more about Singapore:
http://www.sg/kids/
http://www.singaporeport.com/
http://www.excite.com/travel/countries/singapore/
http://www.lonelyplanet.com/destinations/south_east_asia/singapore/

Learn how to make more Singaporean foods:
http://SOAR.Berkeley.EDU/recipes/ethnic/singapore/

Learn more about monsoons:
http://school.discovery.com/homeworkhelp/worldbook/atozscience/m/368780.html
http://www.pbs.org/wnet/nature/monsoon/html/body_make.html